The Second Chance I Gave Myself

From Unanswered Love to Unshakable Self-Worth

Umang Ahuja

Qurate
quratebooks.com

The Second Chance I Gave Myself
From Unanswered Love to Unshakable Self-Worth
Umang Ahuja

Published in 2025

© Published by

urate
quratebooks.com

Qurate Books Pvt. Ltd.
Goa 403523, India
www.quratebooks.com
Tel: 1800-210-6527,
Email: info@quratebooks.com

ISBN: 978-93-5898-866-6

Preface

We all talk about first loves.
Some talk about true love.
But very few talk about what happens **after you've given everything and are left with nothing—**
except yourself.

This book is born from that space.

A space where **unanswered questions, silent exits,** and **quiet sacrifices** pile up inside you
until the only way out is to turn your pain into purpose.

I never imagined I'd write a book.

I'm not an author by profession yet.
I'm someone who lived through everything you're about to read—
from losing my mother in childhood,
to being the student everyone depended on,
to carrying invisible grief while becoming a leader in the professional world, to falling in love with someone who helped me heal...
and then broke me in a way that healed me even deeper.

This is **not just a love story.**

It's a story about **givers**—people like me who love without limits.
People who hold space for others,
but often forget to hold space for themselves.

It's for the ones who've been misunderstood,
the ones who gave too much,
who stayed too long,
who believed too deeply.

And it's especially for those who never got closure,
and had to build peace out of their own pain.

I didn't write this book to change someone's mind.
I wrote it to **clear my own mind and heart.**
I wrote it for every version of me that needed to hear:

"You did the best you could.
And that was enough."

Every chapter in this book is real.
Some names have been changed or omitted for privacy,
but the emotions, the events, the breakdowns and breakthroughs—
they all happened.

And if even one page helps you feel less alone,
or gives you the strength to walk away,
or forgive,
or set boundaries,
or simply love yourself a little more—

Then this book has done its job.

Thank you for holding space for my story.
Now, let's begin.

– Umang Ahuja

Table of Contents

Chapter 1

When Love Left with My Mother

"When a mother leaves too early, something in the child becomes too old, too soon."

I still remember the smell of the schoolbooks I had just wrapped in brown covers, and the excitement of stepping into Class 9. It was supposed to be a new beginning—a new syllabus, new teachers, maybe even a chance to finally make my parents proud.

But just when life was about to open up, it closed something far deeper.

It took her.

My mother.

She didn't leave with words. She didn't say goodbye. She just... vanished into silence.
And in that silence, a boy who still had questions about the world suddenly became familiar with death.

I was too young to understand grief and too old to be comforted by fairy tales.

All I knew was that the woman who once made everything feel safe—her lap, her smile, her scoldings, her prayers—was now only in framed photos and memories that kept fading like sunlight at dusk.

That day changed everything.

My father, broken himself, tried to play the role of both parents. I could see him trying—making breakfast, checking school notes, forcing himself to smile even on the days his eyes gave him away. But love, no matter how well-intended, can't be mimicked.

He wanted to give me the warmth of both mother and father. But what he didn't realize was—you can't double up on one kind of love to fill the absence of another.

It just doesn't work like that.

He gave discipline when I needed understanding and softness.
He offered advice when I craved affection.
And slowly, unknowingly, I learned to quietly shrink my needs.

At school, I laughed when needed. Helped when asked. Smiled on command. I became the "good boy," the "strong one," the one who never broke down—because there was no space for me to fall apart.

At home, things weren't much different.

My sister, older and distant, started mocking me in ways I didn't know how to respond to. "You're adopted," she'd say. "Maa loved me more." It was her way of coping, perhaps. But words, once spoken, don't disappear. They lodge themselves in the corners of a child's heart and make homes out of insecurities.

And mine were growing.
Every taunt became a truth.
Every silence from my father became rejection.
Every moment I craved a hug became proof that maybe I wasn't

worth loving in the first place.

That's the thing about losing a mother—you don't just lose a person.
You lose the **anchor**.
You lose the only person who sees your tears **before** they fall.
You lose the one who makes you feel that no matter what, you're enough.

After she left, I stopped feeling like I was enough.

No one really noticed the change. Because I didn't let them. I wore strength like a uniform—buttoned up, ironed flat, tucked into routine. I became the boy who helped others, the friend who never complained, the student who always scored well.

But deep inside, I was just a little boy standing at the edge of an empty room, whispering, "*Maa, can you come back now?*"

If people ask me today when I started becoming a giver—this was the moment.

This was the origin.

Because when you grow up not receiving the kind of love you need, you either go bitter... or you start giving double of what you never got.

I chose the latter.

I gave more.
I loved harder.
I made sure no one around me ever felt the kind of emptiness I did.

And that's how it began.

Not with romance.
Not with a girl.

But with a loss.

A love that was taken too soon.
A goodbye I never got to say.
A hollow that became my home.

That was the first turning point of my life.

Not the kind you celebrate.
But the kind that quietly changes the course of your soul.

From that day on, I didn't just grow up.
I started building armor.
Smiling through it. Helping through it. Loving through it.
Hoping, just maybe, someday—someone would give me what I had been giving all along.

●●●

Chapter 2

The First Love That Stayed Unspoken

"First love isn't always a relationship. Sometimes, it's a silent lesson written in the language of hope."

It was just another regular school day—bells ringing, students running to their classrooms, the usual hum of chatter echoing across corridors. I was on my way to the staff room to collect some papers for a teacher, carrying the responsibility that had become second nature to me.

That's when I saw her.

She was playing badminton in front of the principal's office—focused, graceful, and completely unaware of the fact that she was about to alter the direction of someone's heart. Mine.

She had this unbothered charm about her. Her laughter floated through the air, untouched by the pressure of studies or reputation. There was something so simple and raw in that moment that it froze me in my tracks.

And just like that, something in me paused.

I had always been the one people relied on. The class monitor, the all-rounder, the student every teacher trusted— the kind who stayed back to solve problems for others, who

led the morning assembly, who made things right when they went wrong.

I was respected. Admired. Even liked by everyone.

But in all of that admiration, I don't think anyone had ever made my heart race quite like she did when she turned, laughing, racket in hand, the sunlight bouncing off her smile like some kind of slow-motion dream.

That moment planted a seed I didn't even know would grow.

She sat in the front row among the girls—sharp, confident, and intelligent. Her answers in class were always thoughtful. Her presence was magnetic. The more I watched her, the more I knew that this wasn't just a fleeting schoolboy crush. It was something deeper.

I wanted to share my world with her. My thoughts, my doubts, my small joys.

For the first time, I didn't want to be the monitor everyone

respected—I wanted to be someone she trusted. So I gathered my courage.

Not once.

Not twice.

Seven times.

That's how many times I expressed my feelings to her. I didn't write poetry or plan grand gestures. Just honest,

heartfelt attempts—each one a little more vulnerable than the last. I never pressured her, never demanded a reply. I just let

her know that someone cared. That someone saw her—not as the pretty girl in the front row, but as a person he wanted to understand.

And all seven times—there was no response.

But I didn't give up. Not because I was desperate, but

because something in me believed in the purity of what I felt. Then, something unexpected happened.

It was just before a long weekend. Some of our mutual friends told her about all the times I'd proposed to her. That Friday, she came up to me, her voice unsure but her eyes steady, and she said:

"*Yes.*"

I was stunned. It wasn't a fairy tale, and yet, it felt like magic. The words didn't echo through the corridors, but in my heart, they danced.

For two days, I lived in a quiet kind of joy.

I didn't tell anyone.

I didn't flaunt it.

I just allowed myself to feel it.

But when Monday came and the school gates opened again, everything had changed.

She took her words back.

No apology. No explanation. Just a quiet retraction, as if those two days had been a mistake that needed erasing.

And what did I do?

I smiled.

And I let her go.

Because I never wanted love that was built on pressure or obligation. I wanted willingness. Sincerity. Something that bloomed naturally, not out of guilt or social nudges.

So I walked away—not because I didn't care, but because I cared enough to give her that freedom.

School went on. Board exams neared. Life moved forward.

And then, one day—out of nowhere—I found out that she was in love with one of my closest friends.

They'd kept it a secret. Hidden it from me, perhaps out of guilt. Maybe they thought I'd be hurt. Maybe they underestimated the kind of heart I carried.

But I didn't react.

Not with anger.
Not with jealousy.
Not with betrayal.

Instead, I silently smiled for them.

Because if she found happiness—even if it wasn't with me—wasn't that what I always wanted for her?

And that's how my first love ended.

It didn't break me.
It shaped me.

Because that chapter taught me more than most relationships ever could. It taught me:

- That love isn't always mutual.
- That feelings can be real even if they aren't returned.

- That silence is an answer too—and sometimes, a gentle one.

More than anything, it taught me about myself.

That I wasn't just someone who loved—I was someone who **loved well.**

With depth. With grace. With dignity.

●●●

Chapter 3

The Hidden Disease Called Depression

"Some wounds don't bleed. They echo—loudest in silence."

People often look at toppers, monitors, the "good kids" and assume they've got it all figured out. From the outside, I still wore the badge of being the favorite student. I still helped others with their studies. Still smiled at teachers, stood first in competitions, and organized school events like everything was fine.

But inside, I was slipping.

And no one knew.

It didn't happen in one single moment.
It was slow, like a leak in the back of your mind that you only notice once the whole floor is flooded.

It started with little things.

I stopped enjoying the songs I once loved.
I avoided group conversations.

My appetite faded—sometimes I overate, sometimes I didn't eat for a whole day.

Sleep became a luxury. Some nights, I stared at the ceiling for hours. Other nights, I fell asleep crying without knowing why.

I couldn't explain it to anyone.

Because *how do you tell someone you're drowning when you look so* functional on the surface?

By the time I reached Class 12, things got worse.

There was pressure from every direction—teachers, relatives, family, society. JEE preparation was in full swing. Everyone was planning their future. And I... I was just trying to hold my present together.

In the middle of pre-boards, I had my first full-blown breakdown.

My heart was pounding, my hands were trembling, and I couldn't breathe. I wasn't crying—but I wasn't stable either. Something inside me had cracked. I left the exam hall midway and went straight to the washroom, locked the door, and collapsed on the floor.

That was the day I first whispered to myself:

"I think I'm not okay."

After that moment, I tried to seek help. But mental health wasn't something openly discussed back then. Especially in middle-class households. Especially for boys.

People said:

"It's just stress. Everyone goes through it."
"Just stay strong. Meditate."
"Don't think too much."

But no one could see the fog I was walking through. Every day.

I didn't want attention. I just wanted someone to ask—not as a formality, but with concern—*"Are you really okay?"*

But that question never came.

So I carried on—quietly battling depression and anxiety that had now settled into my daily routine like an unwelcome roommate.

I somehow completed my boards.

Did I study? Yes.

Did I appear for JEE? Yes.

Did I qualify? No.

And when the results came, there wasn't even disappointment. Just numbness.

My friends celebrated their ranks and admissions. I watched from a distance, smiling at their success, clapping for their photos on notice boards—but inside, I felt like a bystander in my own life.

Eventually, I took admission in a university. Not because I wanted to—but because I had to move forward.

College began. New city, new people, new opportunities.

But one thing remained the same:

The storm inside.

Looking back, that phase taught me one of the hardest truths of life:

You can carry trauma so silently that even you start believing it doesn't exist.

But it does.

And until you face it, it keeps showing up—in your choices, your fears, your relationships, your health.

I was still breathing. Still helping others. Still being the giver. But deep inside, I was just a boy who had forgotten what it felt like to truly be held.

●●●

Chapter 4

New Campus, Old Loneliness

"You can change the city, the clothes, even the nameplate—but not the emptiness you carry inside."

The day I stepped onto my college campus, the sun was brighter, the air felt different, and everything around me buzzed with energy.

It was supposed to feel like a new beginning.

A reset button.

A chance to finally become the version of myself I used to imagine before the storm took over.

But as I walked through the hostel gate for the first time, carrying two bags and a thousand invisible thoughts, I realized—

I had brought all of me with me.

The giver.

The good boy.

The one who listened more than he spoke.

And the one who smiled even when his heart was sinking.

The first semester moved fast—new classes, new faces, new schedules.

But emotionally? I remained on pause.

I made friends easily. I helped everyone with assignments, organized group projects, cracked jokes in class, and even offered emotional support to people I had just met. People liked me. Respected me. Some even admired me.

But no one really *knew* me.

Because the truth was—**I was functioning, not healing.**

I didn't talk about the panic attacks I still got at night. Or how I often walked past my hostel mirror without recognizing the tired boy staring back.

Or how every celebration made me feel lonelier because I didn't know how to be happy anymore.

Then came *her*.

Not with the noise of drama, but with the calm of familiarity. She was soft-spoken, grounded, and had this strange ability to be present without overwhelming. She wasn't like others. She didn't try to fix me. She just listened.

We met during a seminar. Sat next to each other by chance, then bumped into each other again the next day, and again after that.

It started with casual talks—subjects, exams, food.

Then one night, while sitting on a bench under a dim campus lamp, I told her,

"Sometimes I feel like I'm alive for everyone except myself."

She didn't interrupt. She didn't say it would be okay.

She just looked at me and said,

"I'm here. Whenever you need someone to remember you're human."

That night, I didn't cry. But something softened inside me. For the first time in a long time, someone didn't treat my silence as awkward—they treated it as a language.

And so I started letting her in. Slowly.

She saw the cracks I had so carefully plastered. The fatigue in my eyes. The stiffness in my laughter.

I never said I loved her. Not because I didn't feel something, but because I was afraid—

Afraid that I would again give more than I received.

That the pattern would repeat.

That this connection, too, would eventually slip away.

But one part of me hoped—hoped this would be different.

Until the day I saw her holding hands with someone else.

It wasn't dramatic. There were no betrayals, no broken promises.

I had never told her how I felt. She had never made any commitments.

And yet... it felt like grief.

Not because she chose someone else.

But because *I* hadn't chosen *me* first.

I walked away from that moment without confrontation.

No blame. No closure. Just another quiet resignation.

I became the "good friend" again. The one who stayed supportive.

The one who helped others figure out their relationships while quietly failing in his own emotional needs.

But somewhere deep down, I was starting to notice the loop.

I was giving love to people who were never ready to hold it.
I was becoming a healer for others while bleeding inside.
I was still hoping someone would finally choose me… for

me.

College had begun. Life had moved forward.

But the part of me that longed for true, unconditional love— the kind that sees beyond the surface and chooses to stay— remained untouched.

And with every unspoken feeling, every moment I dimmed my needs for someone else's comfort, I realized something deeper:

Being a giver isn't a flaw. But being unseen while giving— that's a slow death.

●●●

Chapter 5

Emotional Burnout and Escapes

"Sometimes, the biggest addictions come from what we're missing, not what we're chasing."

The start of second year brought with it a strange kind of reshuffling.

Our once tight-knit group got scattered across departments—Computer Science, ECE, Mechanical. New classes, new labs, new faces. And somewhere between that logistical split, the emotional closeness cracked too.

Lunch tables changed.
Late-night group studies stopped.
Inside jokes began to fade into awkward greetings.

"We'll meet soon," they said.
But "soon" rarely came.

I stayed available, though.
Always the helpful one. Always the 'yes' guy.

Yes to assignments.

Yes to emotional support.
Yes to being the bridge between disconnected friends.
Yes even when I wanted to scream *"Can someone just ask how I'm doing?"*

But no one did.

And then came the crash.
Not a dramatic one.
Just a slow, quiet unraveling of my inner world.

I started losing sleep.
At first, I blamed stress.
Then I realized it wasn't stress—it was **emptiness**.
That cold, hollow feeling that crawls into your chest at 2 a.m. and refuses to leave.

So I found distractions.

Alcohol.
Drugs.
Not because I loved the high—
But because *they helped me forget the low.*

Just for a while.
Just for a few hours of floating, where pain had no shape and love didn't feel so far.

I told myself I had it under control.

"It's just recreational."
"It helps me sleep."
"Everyone experiments in college, right?"

But deep inside, I knew the truth:
I was escaping.

Not from people.

But from the aching silence that came every time I was alone with myself.

I began working on projects obsessively.

Code. Circuits. Simulations. Anything that made sense when emotions didn't.

My grades improved. Professors appreciated my focus.

People called me ambitious, dedicated.

But they didn't know I was using work to bury my emotions alive.

Because when your reality gets too heavy, you start living in your head.

And that's what I did—**created an imaginary world in my mind.**

A world where I was loved unconditionally.

Where someone waited for me with open arms.

Where I wasn't "the giver"—just someone *held*.

I started having imaginary conversations, reliving memories that never happened, rewriting scenes of life with alternate endings where I mattered more.

Sleep shortened.

Loneliness deepened.

There were nights I stared at the ceiling until morning, not because *I had work—but because I had nowhere safe to rest my heart.*

In front of the world, I was still 'sorted'.

In control. Focused. Disciplined.

But no one knew that the only reason I was surviving college was because I was living somewhere else—in a dream built

inside my mind, far away from a reality that never hugged me back.

And the most dangerous part?

Even I started believing the illusion.

Because it hurt less than waking up to a world that only loved me when I was useful.

By the end of second year, I was emotionally bankrupt. And no one knew.

Because people only notice when the glass breaks loudly. Not when it silently fills with cracks.

But something inside me had begun to whisper now—not loudly, not clearly, but enough to make me pause:

"You can't keep losing yourself just to keep being accepted."

That whisper would grow louder in the chapters to come.

But for now, I was still in survival mode.

Half asleep. Half addicted.
Fully aching.

●●●

Chapter 6

A Voice That Felt Like Home

"Sometimes, the heart finds comfort in someone it's never met—until the world interferes."

Third year began with a quiet promise I made to myself:
No more falling into the same emotional holes.
No more chasing approval.
No more being "available" to the point of exhaustion.

I had just begun pulling myself together—stepping out of late-night drinking, resisting the urge to disappear into imaginary escapes, and focusing instead on my own clarity.

That's when she entered—
Through a phone call.

Not by intention.
Not by design.
Just... accidentally.

She was on a call with my roommate late one evening.
He laughed louder than usual.

They spoke in a comfort language I didn't recognize at first. Then, he said something teasingly and passed me the phone.

"Talk to her. She wants to say hi."

I almost said no. But something in her "hello" stopped me.

Her voice was calm—not bored or flirtatious or trying too hard.

Just real.
Soft.
Gentle.
The kind of tone you only hear when someone speaks without the weight of trying to impress.

We spoke for two minutes.
It felt like ten.
And somehow, it felt like a pause I didn't know I needed.

Over the next few days, it became routine.
She and my roommate had a long-standing bond from school—they were classmates, now self-declared brother- sister types.

She'd call him to catch up. I'd be in the room.
He'd pass the phone for a minute or two.
Our two minutes turned into five... then ten... then late- night conversations of our own.

And without meeting,
without a single shared space or photo,
a connection grew.

She became a voice I waited for.

She asked questions no one else did.
She didn't fill silences—she sat with them.
She didn't offer advice—she offered space.

And in those night-time conversations, something inside me shifted.

I found myself opening up again—slowly, cautiously.

About my sleeplessness.
My burnout.
My emotional messiness.
Even my guilt for giving too much, too often.

She didn't try to fix me.

She just... listened.

And in a world where I had to explain myself to be understood, her silence was louder than most people's words.

For the first time in years, I wasn't performing.
I was just *being*.

And I started to hope—
not for a relationship,
not even for love,
just for *someone to stay.*

But then...
he changed.

My roommate.

He noticed our conversations getting longer.
He started making remarks.

"Bro, she talks to you too much now."
"Don't get too serious, okay?"
"She's family to me. Don't make it weird."

I laughed it off.
I trusted him.
I shared a room with him.
I never once thought he would twist things.

But slowly, things started shifting.

She stopped calling as often.
When she did, our talks were shorter.
Her tone was different—polite, distant.

And then one night, she said something I didn't expect:

"I think it's better we don't talk so frequently. I don't want to make things awkward between you two."

She didn't say it, but I knew.

He had *said* something.
Planted doubts.
Maybe not lies—just enough twisted truth to poison her perception.

And I? I didn't fight for it.

Because I never wanted someone to stay through guilt. After that, it faded.

She stopped calling.
He acted like nothing happened.
Our room felt smaller.
Quieter—but not peacefully so.

And me?
I didn't speak of it again.

Because what hurt wasn't that I lost her.

It was that someone I trusted—*the one who shared my silence, my space, my breath*—chose competition over compassion.

I didn't blame her.

She never promised anything.
She only gave me what she could—her voice.
And for a few weeks, it healed a part of me I didn't even know was bleeding.

But I blamed myself—for hoping again.

Because no matter how calm her voice was,
I forgot the rule that had protected me:

Don't build your peace around people you don't fully know—especially when they're already orbiting someone else's loyalty.

That was the end of the third year.
And the end of that soft hope.

She was never mine.
And yet, losing her felt like something had been taken from me.

Maybe not love.
But something very close to it:

Possibility.

●●●

Chapter 7

The Lockdown Years

"The world shut down, but my loneliness had already begun long before the lockdown."

It started with headlines. Then came panic.

Closures. Empty roads.

And the word that would change life for everyone:

"Pandemic."

I still remember the email:

Final year suspended. College to remain shut. Students to vacate hostels immediately.

It felt surreal. Like we were part of some science fiction film that moved too fast, without a pause button.

Just like that, college was over. Not with farewells.

Not with hugs.

Just silence, backpacks, and unspoken goodbyes. I returned home carrying more than just books.

I carried confusion. Grief.

Unprocessed emotions.

And a heart that hadn't known stability in years.

The world outside was battling a virus.

But I was battling something else: **emptiness.**

Back at home, everything was exactly the same—and yet, nothing felt right.

My father tried to pretend like he was still strong, still

"managing the house."

But he didn't talk much. At least, not to me.

Our conversations revolved around power bills, vegetables, and news updates.

Not once did he ask,

"How are you really holding up?"

He thought being strict was his way of showing care.

He believed putting food on the table meant he had done his job.

But I didn't need food.

I needed affection.

A simple hug. A genuine "I'm here."

And that was the love I never got from him. My mother was long gone.

But in lockdown, her absence echoed in every room louder

than ever.

Every time I passed by the kitchen, I imagined her there. Every evening, when the house grew quiet, I wished I could

hear her voice. Not for answers.

Just for that feeling of being *belonged to.*

But she wasn't there.

And the more I longed for her, the more I realized I'd spent most of my life searching for that same love in every person who came close—and then left.

Then there was my sister.

Living in the same house, speaking the same language, but on an entirely different emotional planet.

She didn't understand me.

Sometimes, I wasn't even sure if she liked me.

Every interaction felt sharp, sarcastic, or just dismissive. She mocked my silence. Called me too emotional. Claimed I was "too dramatic."

And in that house, I became a stranger again.

The first few weeks, I distracted myself with online classes. Then came projects, virtual internships, Zoom lectures.

But slowly… all distractions failed.

Because when you have nowhere to run—**you meet yourself.**

And what I met inside wasn't pretty.

I found fear. Resentment.

A boy still aching for a mother's lap and a father's approval.

A soul tired of being the helper.

A heart that never learned how to be held.

I stopped talking to most people.

Friends called, and I picked up. But I didn't say much.

I became a listener again. The "strong one." The one who

gave pep talks while quietly falling apart.

There were nights when I'd stare at the ceiling, not because I couldn't sleep—

but because I didn't want to wake up to another day that felt

the same.

But amidst all that stillness, I found something I wasn't

expecting.

My escape.

Not through substances. Not through distractions. But through imagination.

I started journaling again. Writing stories in my head.

Building a world where I was loved. Where my mother never left. Where my father held my hand. Where my sister wasn't a stranger.

And in that world, I wasn't lonely.

It was fiction.

But it kept me alive.

Because even though I was physically surrounded by walls,

it was those invisible worlds that gave me breath.

They became my oxygen when no one around me noticed I was suffocating.

That year, I didn't graduate from college.

But I did graduate from illusion.

I stopped expecting people to show up just because they

should.

I stopped explaining my emotions to people who only listened to reply, not to understand.

I stopped waiting for apologies from people who never admitted their absence.

By the end of that lockdown, I didn't become stronger.

But I became clearer. And clarity?

That was more valuable than comfort.

Because now I knew:

Some of us were never meant to be saved by others.

We were meant to rebuild ourselves from every piece that others dropped.

●●●

Chapter 8

Broken Pieces and a New Discipline

"When the world started healing, I began the slow work of rebuilding myself."

By mid-2021, the lockdowns were easing. Shops reopened. Public places came back to life. Students returned to classrooms—some excited, some anxious, some still grieving losses no one talked about.

But me?

Even though the world looked better,

inside, I was still in pieces.

I wasn't broken in a loud, dramatic way.
I functioned.
I submitted assignments.
I cracked small jokes in online group chats.
I even passed exams—which, thanks to the pandemic, were held

in online mode.

But deep down, nothing really felt *right*.

Because the truth was—

The virus had infected everything, including the parts of me I never shared with anyone.

I completed my third year sitting at the same desk where I had cried myself to sleep months earlier.

I gave exams staring into a webcam, answering questions while wearing a blank expression.

I passed, yes.

But I didn't feel victorious.

I felt... *incomplete.*

Still, I told myself:

"This is not where it ends."

When the final year began, something inside me shifted.

Not from inspiration.

Not from a movie or a quote.

But from a **realization** that hit me one morning:

"I don't have the luxury to stay broken anymore."

I wasn't a child.

I was a son—of a father who didn't know how to love me,

but still expected me to succeed.

A brother—though emotionally ignored.

A student—on the edge of being a professional.

And above all, a boy who had carried too much pain to let it win now.

I had reached a point where the **weight of responsibility finally became heavier than the weight of sorrow.**

So I began collecting the broken pieces.

Not perfectly.

Not magically.

But one at a time.

- I forgave myself for not qualifying JEE.
- I stopped begging for emotional presence from people who had no capacity to give it.
- I deleted numbers that only reached out when they needed something.
- I reread the pages of my old journals—not to feel the pain again, but to **understand it**.

And then, I replaced the noise with new voices—**books, lectures, mentors, silence.**

Because healing doesn't always start with hugs.

Sometimes, it begins with **discipline.**

In my final year's first semester, I made a pact with myself:

"Make something good out of this life.

Not because others expect it.

But because you finally believe you deserve it."

I wasn't chasing success anymore.

I was building **stability.**

For my future. For my home.

For the version of me who had endured so much in silence.

Each day became a brick in that foundation.

I woke up early.

Started studying with focus—not panic.

Began networking for job opportunities, not to prove myself, but to prepare for the next chapter.

I exercised—not for a six-pack, but to teach my body it still deserved care.

I prayed—not for miracles, but for **peace**.

And slowly, the fog began to lift.

The flashbacks became quieter.

The triggers lost their sharpness.

The emotional swings turned into steady days.

I wasn't healed.

But I was no longer **helpless**.

And maybe, for the first time in my life, I didn't feel like a wounded boy in an adult's world—

I felt like a man becoming his own pillar.

●●●

Chapter 9

From Survival to Placement

"The world reopened, but I was still putting myself back together."

By the time the world began reopening post-COVID, I looked the same—but I wasn't.

The chaos outside had calmed. Markets reopened, traffic returned, students headed back to campuses. But inside me, a storm still lingered—quiet, constant, and personal.

Everyone around me seemed to have hit "resume."

But I was still buffering—still carrying the weight of the loneliness I had lived through, the silence of a house where love was missing, and the unresolved ache of not being able to ask for more from those I was born to.

Still, I knew one thing with clarity:

This cannot be the story I end with.

It was the beginning of my final year.

And for the first time, I felt something stir inside me—not pain, not anxiety, but **purpose**.

I had spent too long being broken.

Now, it was time to build.

And not for others. Not for validation.

Not to prove myself to the family that never fully understood me.

But for **me**—for the boy who had been carrying dreams in a pocket filled with disappointment for years.

But dreams don't work without resources.

And pocket money was out of the question.

My father, already weighed down by responsibilities, could no longer support my daily expenses. Asking him every week for recharge money, food, or internet felt like begging—not because he made me feel that way, but because **the silence after every "okay, I'll manage" cut deeper than a scolding ever could.**

So I made a decision.

I took up a part-time job—for ₹8000 per month.

It wasn't much.

But it was **mine**.

It meant saying no to hangouts.

It meant working late hours after classes.

It meant eating cheaper food, walking instead of taking rickshaws, skipping sleep to submit assignments.

But it also meant **freedom**.

I was funding my own survival. And that made me stand taller.

While others were focused only on semester marks and college politics, I was quietly chasing stability.

I studied for placement drives. Prepared resumes.

Practiced aptitude tests late at night, often sitting with a fan as my only company.

And by the end of **7th semester**—when many were still unsure of their paths—

I got placed.

A campus placement.

A job offer letter in my inbox.

My name on the selected candidates list. Not with applause.

Not with celebration.

Just a small smile… and a whisper to myself: "You did it. Alone."

That changed everything.

As the 8th semester began, I made a conscious choice:

Instead of attending college regularly, I gave priority to the offer in hand.

I focused on preparing for the job—real work, real responsibility.

And when it came time to submit our final project,

I submitted my **internship file**—the one from real fieldwork, not theoretical fluff.

It wasn't just a submission.

It was a statement.

That I wasn't just a student anymore.

I was becoming a man.

I still carried pain.

My father's affection was still missing.

My sister still kept her distance.

And the absence of my mother still sat quietly in the corner of my heart like a shadow.

But for the first time in years,

I didn't feel like I was losing.

Because I had started **showing up for myself.**

Not as the perfect version. Not healed.

But **functional. Capable. Ready.**

And that's when I realized:

We don't always rebuild ourselves from light.

Sometimes, we build from darkness. From hunger.

From being left out.

From needing to stand because no one came to lift us.

That was the man I was becoming.

Not made of applause, but of quiet grit.

●●●

Chapter 10

The First Taste of Corporate Reality

"The real world didn't wait for healing. It demanded readiness. And I showed up."

The first day of my job wasn't like the movies. No one clapped. No formal welcome kit. Just a simple desk, a login ID, and an unfamiliar silence.

But to me, it was sacred. It wasn't just a job—it was proof that I had made it through the storm.

I didn't have connections. I didn't have luxury. I had grit. And that desk was where that grit was finally allowed to become value.

The early weeks were overwhelming. Everything was new: Corporate etiquette. Technical tools I hadn't used before. And emails—so many emails.

That's where the first real challenge came.

One of my early tasks was to communicate on behalf of our team with an external vendor. I drafted a mail, double- checked it, and hit send.

An hour later, I received a Teams message from my reporting manager:

"Come on call for 5 mins. Need to discuss something."

My heart sank.

On the call, he didn't shout. He didn't insult. But he said

something that pierced quietly:

"Your mail lacks professional tone and confidence. You need to work on your English communication. Start reading. I'll share a book suggestion."

He wasn't wrong. But he wasn't kind either.

It wasn't just feedback—it felt like a spotlight on everything I had tried so hard to fix.

But I didn't react. I didn't explain how I never had polished schooling. I didn't tell him about my ₹8000/month part-time job or my broken home or the pandemic that swallowed half my college life.

I simply said:

"Thank you. I'll work on it."

And I did.

For the next seven days, I rewrote mock emails. I watched YouTube videos on corporate writing. I read the book he recommended. I corrected myself, practiced subject lines, learned when to say "Please advise" and when to close with "Looking forward to your support."

By the end of that week, I was writing mails faster than ever. Clear. Structured. Polished.

On the eighth day, I mailed a report summary to a senior team. Same manager replied in the thread with just one line:

"Well written. Crisp and confident. Good work, Umang."

That wasn't just praise. That was redemption. That's when I truly learned what it means to grow:

Not by defending your weaknesses. But by correcting them silently and letting your progress speak for itself.

The same man who doubted me had now become someone who trusted me.

Not because I argued. Not because I proved a point. But because I delivered.

Every morning after that, I approached my work with a new sense of self. I was no longer just trying to survive. I was contributing. Being seen. Being counted.

The desk where I once sat nervous, now became the desk where I was respected.

I wasn't just building a career. I was building the kind of man

my younger self would have looked up to.

And maybe for the first time in my life, I didn't feel like a giver waiting for love. I felt like a professional delivering value. And being seen—not for my pain, but for my potential.

●●●

Chapter 11

A Brother Found in a Friend

"Some friendships don't begin with laughter. They begin with loyalty."

After a few months into my new job, I was slowly getting into rhythm. My responsibilities grew, and my confidence followed. But deep down, I never forgot where I came from.

And I never forgot who stood beside me when I had nothing.

That's when a call came from someone I hadn't spoken to in a while—a friend from college. We had studied together, survived lectures together, and now, we were walking different paths.

He hadn't received a campus placement. The pandemic had

erased many chances, and life had become heavier for him.

"Bhai, kuch help ho sake to bata... Even contract job chalega. Bas kuch start karna hai."

There was hesitation in his voice. But also hope. Hope that I would understand.

And I did.

Because I had been there—in those shoes. The shoes of asking. The shoes of needing. And if there's one thing I promised myself the day I got my offer letter, it was this:

When I stand, I'll pull someone up with me.

I didn't have to think twice.

I reached out to my HR. Spoke to my reporting manager. Pulled a few strings. Sent his resume. Pushed it like it was my own.

Within two weeks, he got the interview call. And within a month, he joined my company.

The look on his face during our first chai break together at the office cafeteria? Unforgettable.

Two college boys who once sat in dusty benches dreaming of placement drives—now sipping tea as colleagues. As equals.

But what came next was more than work. It was **bonding**. We shared meals. Pulled late-night shifts. Covered for each other. Spoke of our families, losses, goals. We weren't just co-workers.

We became **brothers**.

There were no blood ties. But there was something deeper: Shared struggle. Mutual respect. Quiet loyalty.

He never forgot what I did. And I never let him feel like he owed me.

Because real friendship isn't measured in favors. It's measured in **presence.** In knowing that someone will show up for you—with their time, with their truth.

Over time, people started calling us a team. And we were. Not because we were perfect at work. But because we protected each other outside of it.

When he struggled with tasks, I stayed late to teach him. When I faced criticism, he was the first to message:

"Ignore kar. Tu best kar raha hai."

It was simple. It was real. It was **family without labels.**

Years from now, I may forget the names of many colleagues. But not his.

Because in a world that often rewards competition over compassion, we chose **brotherhood** over everything else.

And that made all the difference.

●●●

Chapter 12

From Trainee to Trailblazer

"Growth isn't about titles. It's about becoming the person who takes ownership when no one else will."

I entered the corporate world as a trainee—one among many. Fresh out of college, eager to prove, ready to learn.

But I was also carrying something different. Not just hunger, but **urgency.**

Not just ambition, but **accountability.**

Because I wasn't working to chase status. I was working to

change my story.

My first designation was simple: Graduate Engineer Trainee. The expectations? Even simpler.

Do what you're told. Learn quietly. Support the team. But I didn't wait to be told.

I started studying existing designs. Volunteering for additional work.

Staying late to understand tools, layouts, approvals, and logic.

Within weeks, my role shifted.

From a supporting hand to a leading one.

From preparing small drawings to designing entire project blueprints.

My seniors noticed.

But I wasn't working for their applause.

I was working for my own growth.

In a few months, I was designing complete projects end-to- end.

Electrical layouts. IBS solutions. Technical documentation. Site coordination. Cross-team communication.

And with every new challenge, I didn't wait for a manager.

I became my own.

When escalations came, I handled them.

When clients asked questions, I answered them.

When deadlines tightened, I stayed through the night to deliver.

I stopped waiting for leadership.

I became leadership.

With time, the stakes grew.

I went from designing local rollouts to managing full-scale projects across multiple zones.

And then came the turning point.

A new Head of Corporate Technology joined our department—**Mr. Ajay Sharma**.

He observed. He assessed. And then, one day, he called me into a meeting and said:

"Umang, I see clarity in your approach and responsibility in

your execution. I want you to take the lead—PAN India." That wasn't just trust.

It was the first time someone in authority didn't just assign

me work—they **believed in me.**

With Mr. Sharma's backing, I was entrusted to:

Lead PAN-India network designing and approvals — with minimal to zero manager intervention. No backup.

No second layer of review.

Just me, a spreadsheet of sites, client expectations, and a national canvas to design.

And I delivered.

Because I didn't see it as pressure.

I saw it as **proof** of who I had become. In this journey, managers changed.

One moved. Another was reassigned.

Some understood my worth. Others didn't.

But Mr. Sharma remained.

He didn't micromanage. He empowered.

And I made sure I lived up to every ounce of his belief in me. Because my **identity wasn't linked to a reporting line.**

It was rooted in my **values**:

- Accountability

- Ownership
- Quiet excellence There were days I felt alone.

Driving approvals, managing pan-India deliveries, coordinating with field teams—all without a second set of eyes.

But I never complained.

Because every time someone asked:

"Who's handling this?"

The answer was always:

"Umang."

And maybe that's what growth really is.

Not waiting for promotions. Not celebrating titles.

But becoming **irreplaceable** through your actions. I started as a trainee.

Today, I lead what others hesitate to even take responsibility for.

Not just because I showed up.

But because someone saw something in me and gave me the chance to **rise.**

And in a world full of people waiting for instruction, I became the one who built direction.

●●●

Chapter 13

The Mentor Who Believed in Me

"Some people don't just lead you—they shape you."

In every professional journey, there comes a point when someone sees in you what even you might not. For me, that person was **Mr. Ajay Sharma**, Head of Corporate Technology.

He didn't just assign tasks. He trusted. He didn't instruct with authority. He guided with purpose. And slowly, what started as a reporting relationship evolved into something far deeper: A **bond**. A connection that blurred the line between manager and mentor, professional and personal.

From the very beginning, I supported him in every assignment he handled. Every document. Every design. Every audit trail. I wasn't just working *under* him—I was building *with* him.

He treated me like a younger brother, not just another resource. And in return, I gave him more than hours—I gave him **commitment**.

We shared jokes during long calls. We stayed up late fixing last-minute compliance issues. We challenged each other to think smarter, push harder, and most importantly, never back down.

One of our most defining moments came during the **company audit**—a transition phase where the company was being acquired by a larger group.

Everything was uncertain. New policies. New leadership. New expectations. But our deliverables? Crystal clear.

We navigated every hurdle—documentation gaps, technical backlogs, and system alignment. Side by side, day after day.

When others panicked, we planned. When the pressure spiked, we stayed calm. And we delivered. Every single audit metric. Every single report.

That phase didn't just test our skills. It proved our synergy.

But not every chapter lasts forever.

Eventually, the winds of change arrived in a form I hadn't expected: **a new manager**. One who saw people as chess pieces, not as teammates. Micro-management replaced trust. Politics crept in where there was once productivity.

Recognition became rare. Frustration became frequent. I had spent **two years** in this company.

From Graduate Engineer Trainee to a fully-fledged Engineer. From nervous onboarding sessions to leading national-scale projects.

But now, I was no longer growing. I was surviving. And I had promised myself long ago:

Never stay in a place that stops valuing your presence.

So, with a heavy heart but a clear mind, I resigned. Not in anger. But with **gratitude.**

Gratitude for the journey. For the learning.

And most of all, for **Mr. Ajay Sharma**.

He wasn't just a department head. He was the mirror that

reflected who I could become.

His belief in me gave me the confidence to lead. His mentorship shaped my values. His friendship made the workplace feel like home.

I left the company that day. But I didn't leave empty-handed. I left with skills, memories, lessons— And the rare gift of having worked with someone who truly **saw me**.

●●●

Chapter 14

Bonds and Boundaries

"Sometimes the hardest thing to leave behind is not a person—it's the version of you that stayed quiet to be accepted."

While my professional life was beginning to stabilize again in a new company, my personal world was quietly collapsing.

Not in loud fights.

Not in obvious betrayals.

But in something much colder—**slow manipulation**.

People I had once called family—friends from college, with whom I had shared food, memories, heartbreaks, and dreams—began to drift.

Not because time pulled us apart, but because **someone pushed.**

She entered like any new face.
Polite. Friendly. Curious.

At first, I didn't think much of it.
She was just another extension of the group.
Someone who joined a little later but was welcomed just the same.

But I started noticing how things were subtly shifting.

Conversations became filtered.
Group chats turned colder.
Plans happened without me.
Inside jokes began feeling like inside *targets.*

And the most dangerous part?

She didn't break the group with confrontation.
She broke it with confusion.

She sowed doubts.
Painted half-truths.
Told them things I never said.
Accused me of thoughts I never had.

And slowly… they believed her.

They forgot how long I had been there.
They forgot who held them during their worst.
They forgot the heart behind every effort I once made for them.

And instead, they began to see me as **the problem.**

"He's emotionally unstable."
"He overreacts to small things."
"He's trying to isolate her."

None of it was true.
But it didn't matter.

In her story, I was the villain.
And in their silence, I was convicted.

I tried to reason.
Tried to remind them of who I was.

Tried to explain the manipulation quietly happening under their noses.

But they weren't listening.
Because when someone whispers long enough in your absence,
Even the most loyal ears start to forget your voice.

And so, I made a decision.

Not out of revenge.
Not out of weakness.

But out of **self-respect**.

I walked away.

I left the group.
Deleted the chats.
Muted the noise.
Let go of the urge to explain myself.

Because I realized something critical:

I can't keep holding onto people who are okay letting me go.

I didn't have time for drama.
I didn't have space for distortion.
And I definitely didn't have the energy to fight for
friendships that chose convenience over character.

I had a **career to build**.
A family name to hold up.

And a **future that couldn't be compromised** by circles that saw my heart as disposable.

But life is beautifully balanced.

Because in the space where some connections broke,
New bonds quietly bloomed.

In my professional world, I began building new relationships. Genuine ones.

Colleagues who respected my work.
Leaders who valued my input.
Peers who didn't care about gossip—only **growth**.

And in their company,
I found what I had missed for years:

Belonging without performance.

No proving.
No pretending.
Just showing up. And being respected for it.

Walking away from people you once called your own doesn't happen in a single moment. It happens in phases:

- First with confusion.
- Then with grief.
- And finally… with peace.

And today, I carry no hatred.
Just a quiet **reminder** of what happens when you stop choosing yourself to be chosen by others.

●●●

Chapter 15

A New Beginning in Delhi-NCR

"A new place doesn't change you. But it gives you a chance to rewrite how you rise."

After walking away from manipulation, lost friendships, and a company where I had given years of my dedication, I found myself at the threshold of something new.

Not just a job.
Not just a company.
But a chance—

To begin again.

I accepted the role of **Associate Engineer – Network Mobility** at one of India's leading telecom operators in the **Delhi/NCR** region.

From the moment I received the offer, I knew this wasn't just about career progression. It was about redemption.

It was about proving—not to others, but to *myself*—that I still had more to give, more to build, and more to become.

My designation came with clarity—

5G Lead for In-Building Solutions (IBS) across high- priority sites.

Alongside me were other associates, each with their own strengths, stories, and struggles.

We were equals on paper.

But I carried something else into this new space—

A fire that had flickered… but hadn't died.

I wasn't here to compete.

I was here to **contribute**.

To find joy in problem-solving again.

To find meaning in systems, diagrams, approvals, and the quiet pride of responsibility.

The first few weeks were filled with onboarding calls, field-level coordination, internal tools, approvals, and 5G design requirements that were evolving faster than anyone could write SOPs for.

But none of that scared me.

Because I wasn't new to pressure.

I was forged in it.

What I was searching for now wasn't just recognition or another star on my resume—

I was searching for **my fire** again.

That inner spark.

That hunger to wake up and do meaningful work.

That fuel I once had in the earlier phase of my career— before it got buried under politics, people-pleasing, and emotional exhaustion.

In this new environment, I made a promise to myself:

"This time, you won't overgive where it's not valued.

You won't chase people.

You'll chase purpose."

And so, I focused—

On listening.

On understanding the core of network mobility from the ground up.

On contributing wherever possible without forcing myself to be visible.

Because I knew—

Excellence doesn't need to shout. It speaks quietly. And people listen.

Colleagues started noticing.

Not for grand gestures.

But for consistency.

For how I handled escalations.

For how I made complex IBS requirements look simpler than they were.

And with every site delivered, every challenge solved, I felt the fire rekindling.

Not in flames.

But in steady warmth.

This chapter wasn't about being the loudest.

It was about **becoming solid**.

I wasn't trying to prove anything anymore.

I was simply doing the work—

Because I respected what I had survived to get here.

In this new company, with new people, I didn't just find opportunity.

I found alignment.

A space where my skills could breathe.

Where my past didn't weigh me down.

And where my future could finally begin to take shape—on my own terms.

●●●

Chapter 16

When Hope Had a Name

"Sometimes, all it takes to remember who you are—is one person walking into your life, unaware of the fire they carry."

It had been six months since I joined the new company.

By then, I had found my rhythm—settled into my role as **5G Lead – IBS**, earned trust, handled critical approvals, and redefined what responsibility meant to me.

But something was still missing.

I had reignited parts of my professional self.
But inside… there was still a silence.
The kind that even achievements couldn't fill.

Until the day **she** walked in.

Her name was **Komal**.

She joined as the **5G Outdoor Lead – Network Mobility**, stepping into a high-responsibility role with the same kind of quiet ambition I had once walked in with.

I still remember the first time I saw her.

It wasn't love at first sight.

It wasn't anything dramatic.

It was just—**a spark**.

A feeling.

That familiar rush in my chest.

The kind that tells you, *"Something just shifted."*

We spoke on her first day. Just small talk.

About tools, team structure, and project alignment.

But her energy was different.

Focused. Grounded. Clear.

She didn't try to impress anyone.

She wasn't loud. But she **radiated presence**.

And something inside me lit up.

In the days that followed, we began talking more.

Sometimes during cross-functional reviews.

Sometimes in lunch conversations.

Sometimes in quiet moments between team calls.

We weren't trying to "connect."

We just *did*.

And without even realizing it,

she became my spark.

Seeing her work with precision made me want to sharpen my own skills.

Her clarity reminded me of the clarity I had buried.

Her discipline became a mirror for mine.

And slowly… the fire I was searching for?

I saw it in her.

And then, I saw it return in myself.

I started taking on more responsibilities—

Not for appraisal.

Not for recognition.

But because I was inspired.

By her consistency.

Her calm.

Her focus.

And yes—by the way her presence made even the toughest days feel *lighter*.

She never tried to fix me.

She didn't even know I needed fixing.

But her being there was enough. To make me sit straighter.

To show up sharper.

To lead like I used to—**but better.**

And in all of that… **hope returned.**

Not just for love.

But for *life*.

For the kind of bond that doesn't pressure you to become someone else—but reminds you of who you are at your best.

Komal may never know the full depth of what she brought into my world.

But I know this:

She didn't just walk into the office one day.

She walked into my story.

And lit up the pages I had forgotten how to write.

•••

Chapter 17

Taking the Lead

"Sometimes it takes just one person to look you in the eye and say— "You're ready." And suddenly, you are."

I had been delivering consistently.

Site after site.

Solution after solution.

Designs completed.

Approvals aligned.

Team escalations managed without delays.

The spark had returned.

My confidence was climbing.

And my sense of ownership? Unshakable.

But one thing was still missing—**recognition that moved me forward.**

Until the day **Mr. P.** , my manager, called me into a brief discussion and changed everything.

He had been observing quietly.

Watching the way I handled cluster escalations,

How I closed IBS project loops without reminders,

How I maintained network mobility designs under pressure without needing backup.

And then he said something I'll never forget:

"Umang, you've got it in you. Not just to follow. But to lead.

Start taking full charge. I trust you completely.

Build your future from this."

It wasn't a long speech.

It didn't need to be.

Because in those few words, he gave me something most people spend years waiting for:

A push with purpose.

That very day, I shifted gears.

I stopped waiting for approvals before taking action.

I stopped depending on layers of confirmation.

I took **full leadership and accountability** of every IBS project in the **Delhi/NCR** region.

No micro-management.

No second opinions.

Just **trust, execution, and results.**

My role evolved from **Associate Engineer** to **unofficial project lead**—managing complete IBS lifecycles:

- Technical solution designing for both indoor and outdoor mobility.

- Coordination with vendors and cluster teams.

- Troubleshooting interference, design mismatches, or escalation delays.
- Timely approvals through central teams and management platforms.
- Delivery assurance for high-priority locations like malls, hospitals, airports, and commercial hubs.

I handled not just data—but **decisions**.

And the best part?

Mr. P. never hovered.
He empowered.

In his management style, I found the balance I had always respected—

Firm when needed, but always **backing belief over fear.**

His leadership reminded me of Mr. Ajay Sharma from my previous company.
Both were cut from the same rare cloth:

Leaders who don't compete with you—they grow you.

And in that space, I grew.

By now, I wasn't just leading IBS work across Delhi/NCR— I was mentoring new associates, supporting team-level escalations, and even collaborating with national leads on future rollouts.

Every time I was asked,

"Who's handling this site?"

The answer stayed the same—

"Umang Ahuja."

And that name now stood not just for responsibility— But for **results.**

Looking back, I realized it wasn't a designation that made me a leader.

It was a choice.

A decision to take complete ownership and stop seeking permission to rise.

And it all started with a sentence from a manager who saw something in me,

long before I had the courage to claim it fully myself.

●●●

Chapter 18

Silently Saved

"Sometimes, it's not a loud voice that pulls you out of darkness. It's a quiet presence that reminds you of the light you forgot you carried."

Progress isn't always professional.

Sometimes, the biggest milestones are the ones no one sees.

Yes, I was leading IBS solutions across Delhi/NCR.

Yes, I was earning the trust of my seniors.

Yes, I was becoming the guy people counted on.

But there was still something I hadn't told anyone.

I was still haunted by old habits.

Not as visibly.

Not as destructively.

But still there—drinking to silence the noise,

Carrying the memory of substances that had once helped me cope with emptiness.

The world was watching my growth.

But inside, I was still healing from being unseen for so long.

And then came **Komal**.

Not like a fixer.

Not like a savior.

But like **a mirror**—of who I could be.

She never said it outright.

She never lectured me on my past.

She never even asked about the darker corners of my story.

She just… **showed up**.

Every day. With calm. With grace. With the kind of grounded energy that made everything else in the room feel a little more stable.

There were moments I sat across from her after a long day, still carrying the weight of old thoughts—

an urge, a trigger, a habit I hadn't completely shaken off.

And she would just smile.

Not to impress.

Not to distract.

Just a simple, honest smile that carried more power than any therapy session ever could.

It gave me **chills**.

Not out of fear.

But because it reminded me—

This is what peace looks like.

And if she could carry that,

I could learn to carry it too.

Without saying a word, Komal became my accountability.

Not by pressure.

But by presence.

Her silence taught me more than most advice ever had.

Because when someone believes in your light —

even without understanding your darkness —

you begin to believe in it too.

And then there was **Mr. P.**

A man of clarity.

Of conviction.

He didn't just manage my work—he **mentored my mindset**.

In meetings, in one-liners, in small nudges to take on more leadership,

he made me feel like someone who could rise further—*not in position, but in purpose.*

Between Komal's quiet strength and **Mr. P's** faith in my potential,

I stopped chasing the need to escape. And started building the strength to stay.

Stay present.

Stay sober.

Stay steady.

I still remember the day I threw out the last reminder of that chapter—

the bottle I kept "just in case."

It wasn't a big scene.

No emotional speech.

Just a whisper to myself:

"She deserves better.

He expects more.

And I'm finally ready to give both."

That was the day I reclaimed a part of myself I had long buried—
The disciplined, focused, emotionally awake version of me.

The version that no longer needed pain as a crutch.

The version that was no longer hiding behind chemicals or distractions.

The version who could now walk into a room—

look at Komal…

look at my manager…

and most importantly,

look at myself—without shame.

●●●

Chapter 19

The Jealousy That Followed

"Not everyone claps when you rise—especially the ones who once led you."

Success comes with its own kind of silence.

In the beginning, people cheer.
They support you, mentor you, guide you.
They praise your passion and your dedication.
But when your growth starts outpacing their comfort—
support becomes resistance.

And that's exactly what happened.

By now, I had made a mark in the team.
IBS design and execution across Delhi/NCR was flowing under my leadership.
From escalations to approvals, from planning to final submission—

I was owning every loop.

My work started getting recognized beyond my immediate circle.
Senior leaders noticed.

And slowly, without even trying,

I began reporting directly to the Head of the Network Mobility Planning Team.

It wasn't out of disrespect.

It wasn't a power grab.

It was simply the **natural outcome of delivering value where it mattered most.**

But not everyone saw it that way.

My manager, who once encouraged me to take charge, suddenly began to change.

His tone became colder.

His instructions became fewer.

And the warmth that once marked his guidance… disappeared.

It wasn't said directly, but it was **loud in the silence**:

"You've gone too far. Too fast."

Meetings that used to be collaborative turned stiff.

My suggestions were questioned—not for quality, but to regain control.

My decisions, once celebrated, were now filtered through doubt.

At first, I tried to overlook it.

I stayed respectful.

I kept him in the loop.

I credited him where due.

But it became clear—**this wasn't about process.**

It was about **ego.**

The very leadership he once pushed me toward…

Now made him uncomfortable.

And soon, he began withdrawing support altogether.

- Ignoring escalations where I needed his backup.
- Keeping me out of discussions I should've been
- leading.
- Subtly redirecting my efforts, just to slow things down.

It wasn't sabotage.

But it was suppression.
And it hurt—not because I couldn't handle it,
but because **he was once someone I respected deeply.**

I had a choice to make:

- Dim my fire to protect his insecurity.
- Or keep walking toward the light I had worked so hard to earn.

And I chose the latter.

Because I wasn't chasing positions—I was **protecting purpose.**

Yes, it was difficult.
Yes, I felt the weight of silent resentment.
But I reminded myself:

"You didn't come this far to shrink back for someone else's comfort."

I didn't skip steps.
I didn't cheat the system.
I just delivered—consistently, quietly, relentlessly.

And if that's threatening to someone?

That's a reflection of **them**, not me.

Ironically, as his distance grew,
the trust from higher leadership deepened.

I didn't seek a title.
But I earned their confidence.
Not through politics —
Through **proof**.

Proof of performance.
Proof of accountability.
Proof that leadership isn't always about position—
It's about ownership.

And through it all, I carried one lesson with me:

Sometimes, your growth will cost you relationships you thought were unshakable.
But never let that stop your evolution.

●●●

Chapter 20

The Distance Within

"In a world where egos clash and insecurities speak louder than talent, sometimes all you need is one calm soul to remind you who you are."

The days were getting heavier.

I was still delivering.
Still leading IBS designs across Delhi/NCR.
Still reporting directly to senior leadership, managing approvals, planning, escalations, timelines.

But in the shadows—**the resistance was growing.**

My manager, once supportive, had now turned cold.
His tone no longer carried mentorship.
His eyes carried discomfort every time someone above praised my name.

Every day, a new hurdle surfaced:

- A missed mail loop he "forgot" to include me in.

- A review he redirected to someone else just to make me chase closure.
- A subtle jab in meetings: *"Let's make sure Umang isn't overstepping again."*

It wasn't open conflict.

But it was **emotional erosion**.

And it started to get to me.

I'm not made of stone.

Even with self-awareness, there are moments where silence screams louder than words.

And for a while—I started questioning myself.

Was I doing too much?

Was I wrong to take initiative?

Was it my fault he felt threatened?

That kind of self-doubt can be more dangerous than any professional escalation.

But just as that heaviness started creeping in...

Komal kept showing up.

She didn't fight my battles.

She didn't even know every detail.

But she had this ability—

To pull me back to myself with nothing more than a glance.

On days I'd return from back-to-back reviews with stress on my face,

she'd look up and just say:

"You still haven't eaten, have you?"

That was her way of saying:
"You're not alone."

Her calm was disarming.
Her smile? A reset button.
Her presence? A reminder:

"You are still you. Even if someone else can't handle your light."

While the world tested my patience,
Komal became my grounding.

She didn't give me solutions.
She gave me space.
To breathe.
To reflect.
To **feel enough—without doing more.**

And slowly, I began to detach from the emotional weight of my manager's jealousy.

Not by retaliating.
Not by proving a point.
But by doing what I do best:

- Delivering clean.
- Leading smart.
- Building forward.

I turned the noise into **focus**.
The silence into **fuel**.

And I let Komal's presence—not her words—remind me of a truth I had forgotten:

"You don't need validation from those who compete with you. You need alignment with those who believe in you."

That's what she gave me.

In every quiet laugh.
In every shared chai break.
In every unspoken look that said:

"Keep going. I see you—even when others pretend not to."

With her by my side, I became more of me.

Not just a network engineer.
Not just a project lead.
But a man who was finally learning to navigate pressure with **peace.**

Because real strength isn't shown by dominating others—

It's shown in how calmly you walk forward when others try to pull you back.

●●●

Chapter 21

Seeds of Separation

"There's no storm more dangerous than the one that whispers lies in the ears of those who once trusted you the most."

Every bond that's built in truth eventually faces its test.

And mine with **Komal** was no different.

Ours was never loud.
Never romanticized or rushed.
It was something else entirely—

A friendship built in silence.
A bond that didn't demand space, but created it.

But when people who fear authenticity see two souls quietly aligned,

They start to panic.

Especially when one of them can't be controlled.

By now, I had become a lead in action, even if not by title. Managing projects independently, reporting to senior management, driving IBS execution across Delhi/NCR without intervention.

It didn't sit well with my immediate manager.

He saw the influence I carried.
He felt the respect I was earning.

And worst of all?

He noticed **the quiet connection** I shared with Komal.

So instead of confronting me…
He did something worse.

He invited someone into the circle.
A person from my past.

Someone who knew how to wear warmth like a costume. Someone who had once used their proximity to me for subtle advantage. Someone who knew exactly where to insert doubts.

She re-entered under the guise of "team coordination."
But her presence was anything but neutral.

She didn't confront.
She whispered.
She didn't accuse.
She suggested.

And Komal—sensitive, intelligent, intuitive Komal—began to feel the pull of confusion.

Not because she was weak.
But because **manipulation doesn't scream. It seduces.**

Suddenly, things changed.

Not drastically. But enough.

Our effortless laughter now paused before it flowed.
Our daily rhythm began to stagger.
Conversations got shorter.
Messages slower.

And it wasn't because she had changed.
It was because **the story about me had changed in her ears.**

The woman from my past was seeding quiet doubts. And my manager was giving her space to do it.

Both had found common ground in their discomfort toward me.
Not because I did wrong.
But because I had risen too far **outside their control.**

There were moments where Komal looked at me, and I saw the conflict in her eyes.

Like she wanted to believe what she always knew about me— but another voice was speaking louder now.

A voice that said:

"Maybe he's too intense."
"Maybe he's manipulating you emotionally."
"Maybe he just wants to keep you dependent."

None of it was true.
But truth rarely survives unchecked repetition.

Still… I didn't push back.
I didn't confront the woman.
I didn't fight the manager.

Because I've learned —

You don't battle shadows.
You stand in your light and let the truth stay visible.
Even if it flickers.

And so, I stayed the same:

- Consistent.
- Quietly supportive.
- Present, even in distance.
- Respectful, even in heartbreak.

Because I knew—if the bond was real, it would find its clarity.

And if it wasn't, then I was never truly seen in the first place.

What hurt most wasn't the coldness from above.
I had seen that before.

It was the shifting energy of someone who once made me believe I could heal.

But I also knew this:

Some people come into your life to awaken you—
not to stay forever,
but to show you what you deserve to feel.

And **Komal had already done that**—whether she stayed or not.

So I walked forward.

Not in anger.
Not in pain.
But with the quiet dignity of someone who's been misunderstood…
but never misplaced his truth.

●●●

Chapter 22

The Weight of Society

"Sometimes it's not love that ends a bond—it's fear dressed as logic, and society whispering louder than the heart."

For a long time, none of it mattered.

Not age.
Not expectations.
Not who was ahead in which part of life.

We were just **two people**,
finding calm in each other,
building something without labels,
without promises—just presence.

But eventually, the world caught up.
And with it came all the **questions we had been too whole to ask before.**

It started in moments too subtle to catch.

A longer pause before replying.
A hesitation in her eyes when our names were mentioned together.
A sense of distance—not in kilometers, but in conviction.

The same girl whose presence once pulled me out of old habits, who smiled without needing explanations,

who made me believe I could be **more of myself** without apology…

She was slowly pulling away.

And it wasn't personal.
Not in the cruel way.

It was societal.
It was circumstantial.
It was **practical**.

The kind of emotional pull-back that doesn't scream—

"I don't care about you."

It quietly whispers—

"I care about you too much to let this hurt later."

The things we never spoke of were now sitting between us.

- The age gap.
- The difference in our emotional timelines.
- The unequal weight of responsibility.
- The fear of being misunderstood by the world we both had to live in.

I was already carrying the pressure of family, career, survival. And she… she was just beginning to **find her wings.**

And maybe, deep down, she knew:

"To fly free, she couldn't carry my weight too."

Even if I never asked her to.
Even if I never expected her to.

People around us began to notice.
To comment.
To speculate.

And slowly, the idea of "us" became heavier than the feeling of "us."

And that's what broke me the most.

Not that she stopped feeling.
But that she felt **too much of the world's noise**
and too little of the quiet truth we had built.

There's a pain that doesn't come from betrayal.
It comes from **being outgrown emotionally by someone who once found home in your heart.**

And that's the pain I carried.

She didn't leave with drama.
There were no harsh words.
No ending text.
No final call.

Just a slow fading—
like the volume being turned down on a song you never wanted to stop.

And yet, I understood.

Because real love isn't about holding someone in place. It's about holding space for them—even if that means **letting them go.**

But if she ever wonders...
If she ever sits in silence and remembers—

I hope she knows this:

"You weren't a distraction.
You were direction.
You didn't delay me.
You reminded me of my light.
And if the world made you forget it—
I'll still remember for both of us."

●●●

Chapter 23

The Trip That Changed Everything

"There are places where love is not spoken but felt, where silence says more than speech—and where, sometimes, the one meant for you forgets how to listen."

It was just the three of us.

No crowd.
No workplace noise.
No professional masks.
Just a spontaneous trip to **Vrindavan—**
the sacred ground where Radha's love became legend, and Krishna's flute still echoes through hearts that know silence.

I didn't go there as a tourist.
I went as a seeker.

And deep inside, I believed this trip wasn't just a break— It was **a sign.**

An alignment.

A sacred mirror to show us what we truly were.

With Komal beside me, the energy shifted.

Not just in the surroundings.

But within me.

The city seemed to breathe in rhythm with us—

from the morning aartis to the crowded lanes of Banke Bihari, to the quiet stillness near the Yamuna.

There were moments I looked at her and felt—

This is what peace tastes like.

This is what divinity feels like when it enters your life in human form.

She didn't need to say anything.

Her presence was enough.

Her stillness was grounding.

Her smile, though quiet, lit something in me that even years of self-doubt couldn't touch.

And yet, in that same divine atmosphere, something darker was at play.

Not a fight. Not a disagreement.

But a **subtle shift.**

Because the third person on that trip didn't just come to visit temples—

They came with **a purpose.**

A quiet one.

A calculated one.

The kind of energy that sees something pure and tries to taint it without leaving fingerprints.

Words were softly planted.

- *"You're younger, you should think more clearly."*
- *"Maybe this connection is too deep, too soon."*
- *"He's in a different life phase. Are you sure this won't hold you back?"*

They weren't loud suggestions.
They were whispers—
tailored perfectly to Komal's doubts,
wrapped in the false concern of a "well-wisher."

And slowly, I felt her slip.
Not in body.
But in energy.

Her eyes lingered on me, but not with ease anymore.
Her voice softened, but not with intimacy—**with distance.**

That night, standing outside Prem Mandir,
I felt the most beautiful pain I had ever known:

The universe was showing us something eternal...
And she was walking away from it.

I didn't argue.
I didn't beg.
I stood in the glow of that temple and offered my truth the only way I knew how—
through stillness.

Because Vrindavan doesn't test you with noise.
It tests you with clarity.

And it was clear:

This wasn't a coincidence.

This was sacred.

But sacred things are easy to doubt when the world has taught us to fear what we cannot control.

She didn't leave me that day.

But part of her trust did.

And it wasn't her fault.

The fear wasn't hers alone.

It had been fed.

Nurtured by someone who saw what we had— and didn't want it to survive.

That day, Vrindavan whispered truth to both of us.

But only I stayed to listen.

●●●

Chapter 24

A Proposal Met with Delay

"Sometimes the most courageous thing you can do is love someone not just for who they are—but for the pain they hide, and the peace they deserve."

I never planned to propose.

Not then. Not like that.

But sometimes, when you see someone slipping— not because they want to,

but because **the world is pulling them away**— you don't wait for the perfect moment.

You speak your truth before it gets silenced by everyone else's version of her story.

And so I did.

With all the sincerity I carried.

With none of the performance.

"Will you marry me?"

Not because I wanted a yes.

But because I wanted to offer **her a shelter** from the storm.

A place to rest.
A bond untouched by noise.
A decision rooted not in pressure, but in **peace**.

But I also knew what I was up against.

I was younger.
Not just in age—but in how people measured "readiness."
She was established, focused, practical.
I was still evolving—passionate, emotional, and above all, sincere.

And in the eyes of others, that sincerity wasn't strength.
It was *naivety*.

To them, I wasn't someone worthy of her.
I was someone **getting in her way.**

The manipulation had already begun.

From our manager.
From someone close to her who disguised control as care.

And while Komal never admitted it directly,
I could see her struggling—

- Between what she **felt** and what she was being told to fear.
- Between the **bond** we had and the **labels** the world was ready to place on it.
- Between the **fire in her heart** and the **pressure on her shoulders**.

So when she replied, her voice was calm… but distant:

"Give me 12 months. I'll answer you after that."

And I understood immediately—
It wasn't a promise.

It was an attempt to pause something
she was no longer being allowed to feel freely.

We weren't in the same company anymore.

I had accepted a new role.
An offer that aligned with my values, my pace, and the silence I needed to grow.

She was still waiting—
For a new opportunity, yes—
But also for **clarity**,
for space away from the voices that were shaping her decisions.

And in that space, I made my own choice:

To protect her, like she once protected me.
Not with force.
Not with pressure.
But with **presence**—even from a distance.

Because I had seen her wounds.
The kind that don't bleed, but shape how a person loves.

And I couldn't walk away from them.
Not when she had once stayed through mine.

Maybe she won't remember how I looked at her that day.
How steady my voice was.
How unshaken my intent felt.

But I will always remember **why** I asked her to marry me.
Not to own her.
But to offer her something no one else was willing to give:
Freedom. Without fear.

●●●

Chapter 25

The Wounds Behind Her Walls

"Sometimes love is not about holding hands. It's about holding space—for someone to come back to themselves, even if they're being pulled away from you."

It didn't surprise me when it happened.

I had seen it coming

—long before the words were said, long before the steps were taken.

Right after I proposed to Komal, her friend took her on a trip.

Not just a casual outing.

It was **strategic**.

A carefully timed escape,

engineered to distance her from the very thing that made her feel safe—**us.**

I don't say this with bitterness.

I say it with the calm of someone who has seen this play out before.

When people can't control your spirit,
they try to isolate the one who gives you strength.

And in this case, I was that strength for Komal.
Not by force.
But by presence.
By understanding her silence.
By loving her through her shadows.

But her friend knew that.

She knew our bond wasn't surface-level.
It was soul-deep.
It was growing past the limits others were comfortable with.

So the trip came.

A distraction.
A recalibration.
A moment designed to **plant a seed—**

"You need to move on."
"He's too young."
"You're not the same."
"Think about your career."

It was subtle.
But it worked.

Not because Komal didn't love me.
But because **her mind was exhausted**.

And that's the tragedy, isn't it?

Her body knew the peace she felt around me.
Her soul had already found alignment with mine.

But her **mind—**

the part that had been trained to listen to logic, labels, and external validation—

refused to surrender.

She didn't walk away out of doubt.

She walked away because she was **taught to doubt what's real.**

And I… I knew all of this.

From the moment she told me about the trip,

From the shifts in her tone when she came back,

From the way she began over-explaining things she never used to explain.

I knew the seed had been planted.

But I also knew something else—

I still wanted to help her heal.

Even if it cost me **my emotions**.

Even if it left me alone with the very pain I had once buried because of her.

Because this wasn't just about love anymore.

This was about **honor**.

How could I walk away,

when I had seen the parts of her no one else cared to acknowledge?

The overthinking.

The pressure to be perfect.

The exhaustion of being the responsible one all the time.

I remembered one evening when she was exhausted beyond words.

She didn't say it, but her eyes told me—

She just wanted someone to sit with her and not expect her to be anything.

So I sat.

No questions.
No comfort.
Just presence.

And she leaned back, closed her eyes, and whispered—

"I don't know why, but I feel safe around you."

That moment wasn't imagined.
That energy wasn't fiction.
That bond wasn't in my head.

It was **real**.

But sometimes, real isn't enough to silence **external voices**.

So I let her go.
Not in resentment.
But in respect—

For her process.
For her confusion.

For the girl who once helped me rise, and now needed help herself.

And if that help came at the cost of my own emotional peace, So be it.

Because love, at its core, is not about receiving.
It's about protecting—even when you're not the one being chosen.

●●●

Chapter 26

The Hidden Resume

"Real maturity isn't proving your love—it's protecting someone's growth, even when they don't recognize your hand behind the light they walk toward."

There was a day—quiet, almost forgettable to the world— when she looked me in the eyes and said:

"I just need someone who's mature enough to understand where I am in life."

She wasn't accusing.
She wasn't even aware of how deeply those words struck.

Because what she didn't know was—
I had already given her that maturity.

Long before she asked for it.
In silence.
In sacrifice.
In **choosing not to be seen**, just so she could grow without feeling owed.

She had been struggling to get her next job.

Her resume—rushed, flawed, outdated—was getting rejected everywhere.

I knew.

She never had to tell me.

The girl who once helped me build my professional voice was now losing hers in the world of algorithms, applications, and unanswered HR calls.

And I couldn't stand by.

But I also knew this:

If she found out I was helping…

She would pull away.

Not out of ego.

Out of guilt.

Because Komal wasn't ungrateful.

She was **guarded**.

So I did what real love does when it knows it can't stay in the

light:

I helped her **in the dark.**

She had shared an old version of her resume once— months ago, casually, without expectation.

I remembered every flaw.

Every formatting issue.

Every misplaced detail that could cause a system to reject her.

So I rebuilt it.

Not for credit.

Not for a thank you.

But because I couldn't sit and watch someone drown when I had already learned how to swim through rejection myself.

It was February.

She was trying—hard.

Each rejection chipped at her confidence in small, invisible ways.

And I watched.

Silently.

Creating the very tool that would one day **reopen her door to hope.**

She never knew.

Because I made sure she wouldn't.

Because she asked for maturity.

And this—this quiet act—was **my version of it**.

Not telling her what I did.

Not waiting for her to ask for help.

Just giving it—

as a gift wrapped in distance.

Because if she knew,

she would have stopped me.

Or worse—she would have felt like she owed me something.

And **love isn't a transaction.**

Not when it's real.

Some days I felt the ache of her absence more than I wanted to admit.

But on those days, I reminded myself:

Helping her, even from afar,
wasn't weakness.
It was worship.
A quiet prayer sent through action.
A form of devotion without expectations.

In her eyes, I might've been the one who stayed behind.

But in reality—
I was the one **clearing the path ahead**, just out of sight.

And maybe one day, she'll realize:

The resume that finally got her the job...
Wasn't just a document.

It was a chapter of **unseen love.**

●●●

Chapter 27

A Legacy Left in Silence

"You don't leave to escape.
You leave to uplift.
Because a true departure isn't marked by absence—
but by what you leave behind glowing."

My last working days were drawing close.

And while most people spend their final weeks counting hours,

I was counting **opportunities**.

Not for myself—
but for those I could still lift before walking away.

This exit wasn't about letting go.
It was about **letting rise**—others, processes, energy.

Because if there's anything life had taught me by now, it was

this:

When one thing leaves your life,
another is always waiting—
if you make space for it with grace.

There was a company—
their invoice had been stuck for over a month.

Emails ignored.
Calls unanswered.
Delays that piled up like silence in a broken bond.

And I could've walked away without touching it. But something in me said:

"No. Clear the path for someone else to breathe easier."

So I took it up.

Navigated the process.
Resolved the delay.
Got the invoice cleared.
No friction. No noise.

And then—
I transferred the credit to the name of my former manager.

The same one who once withheld support, played politics,
and made growth heavier than it needed to be. Why?

Because growth doesn't mean revenge.

It means you're no longer bound to the version of yourself that needed validation from people who never saw you clearly.

But it didn't end there.

There was also **her friend**—the one who had once echoed whispers meant to create distance between Komal and me.

But I didn't hold that against her.

Instead, I introduced her to someone **new**.
A young woman—fresh energy, raw talent, and a thirst to learn.

And I said to her friend:

"Guide her.
Train her.
What you once used to pull someone down, now use to lift someone else up."

Not out of instruction.
But as an invitation—
to grow beyond the past,
and become a guide instead of a gatekeeper.

In that moment, I saw her pause.

The years between them were obvious—

the new girl was way younger, filled with eagerness and curiosity.

But that's what made it powerful.

Because often, **life gives you a second chance—**
not through the same person,
but through someone who reminds you of what you could've been
if you had chosen differently.

And maybe, just maybe—
she saw herself again.

Not as a manipulator.
But as a **mentor.**

These last few actions weren't grand.
They weren't posted.
They weren't even spoken about.

But they mattered.

Because I wasn't just leaving a company.

I was leaving behind:

- Resolved debts.
- Redirected energy.
- Opportunities passed on with love, not bitterness.

Some people leave with resignation letters. Others leave with restoration.

I chose the latter.

And as I packed the last of my belongings,

I didn't feel empty.

I felt **whole**.

Because even though one chapter was ending,

I hadn't walked away from it.

I had **walked through it—**
with grace, clarity, and the quiet satisfaction of knowing...

Sometimes, the best closure you can give yourself is becoming the kind of ending you wish others had offered you.

●●●

Chapter 28

The Farewell and the Signs

"Sometimes, the last thing you say isn't for closure.
It's to protect someone from everything they'll face once you're gone."

It was my last day at work.

The final login.
The final call.
The final room I'd walk out of as an employee— but not as the man they'd grown to respect.

The air felt heavy.
Not with sadness,
but with **meaning**.

Everyone had known this was coming.
But none of us were truly ready for it.

As I walked through the corridors,
people paused.
Some smiled faintly.

Some looked away to hide the tears in their eyes.
Some came forward—
handshakes turning into unexpected hugs.

Because I hadn't just completed projects.
I had created **connections.**

With discipline, yes.
With deliverables, of course.

But more than that— with **presence**.

In a world full of employees,
I had chosen to be **a person** first.

And then came the last moment:
my farewell speech.

I stood there, heart full but voice steady.

No bitterness.
No dramatics.
Just the truth:

"Work is never about the designation.
It's about the impact.
And if I've been able to ease your load,
or inspire your steps,
then I leave fulfilled."

There were no applause breaks. No interruptions.

Just silence—
the kind that only comes when words carry truth too deep to be immediately processed.

I scanned the room.
Faces blurred behind emotion.
Except one.

Hers.

Komal stood there.
Silent.
Still.
Watching not just a colleague leave— but **a part of her emotional anchor**.

And in that moment, I remembered:

Her offer letter hadn't arrived yet.

She still had time to serve.
Time to survive.
Time to face the very people who had once shaped her confidence into confusion.

And I knew—

She was not ready.
Not for what would follow my exit.

So I did what I had to.

I said something—
not cruel,
not false,
but strategically placed.

Something subtle.
A sentence she wouldn't question at first...
but that would keep her **distracted just enough** to shield her from the storm coming.

Because the people around her still carried the same intent. The same manipulation.

The same pressure masked as protection.

And she—soft, loyal, self-sacrificing—would absorb it all. Unless I gave her something else to focus on.

And so I planted it.
Not a lie.
But **a misdirection**.

Just enough to create space for her to breathe,
to not overanalyze every glance,
to avoid emotional damage while waiting for that offer letter to finally arrive.

Because love isn't always about honesty.

Sometimes, it's about **strategic silence**.
About choosing what to say—
not for yourself,
but for someone else's protection.

After the speech, people came one by one.
Messages.
Gratitude.
"I've learned so much from you."
"You always made the impossible feel manageable." "You never made me feel small."

And all I could do was smile.

Because what I left behind wasn't just systems or reports—

I left behind **calm.**
I left behind **trust.**

And then I walked out.

One step. Then another.
No backward glance.

Not because I didn't care.
But because I knew—

The seeds I'd planted would bloom.
Some into growth.
Some into **protection.**

Especially hers.

And when her offer letter arrives,
as I know it soon will—
maybe she'll look back and realize:

He never abandoned me.
He just left early…
to clear the way.

●●●

Chapter 29

The Blocked Roads to Her Heart

"Sometimes you don't keep showing up because you're stubborn. You do it because you know healing doesn't arrive in a moment— it begins when one person refuses to give up, even when the other turns away."

The call came.

The one she had waited months for.
The one she deserved.
The one I knew was on its way—**her job offer finally arrived.**

And as soon as I heard the news,
my heart didn't hesitate.

Not for attention.
Not for credit.

Just a pure, unshaken intention:

To be there for her.
To celebrate this chapter she had earned.
Even if she no longer celebrated my presence in hers.

I planned to visit her.

Nothing dramatic.
Just a quiet show of support.
A small gesture to remind her:

"Even if we've drifted,
your wins still matter to me."

But when I arrived…
she was different.

Her energy had changed.

Not angry.
Not bitter.
Just… distant.

Her eyes didn't search for mine like they used to. Her words, though polite, were no longer personal. Her body was there—but her mind was elsewhere.

She had **other plans.**
Other conversations.
Other people who now had her time.

And maybe I should've taken that as my cue to leave.

But I stayed.

Because real love doesn't run from silence.
It listens to what isn't being said.

The next day, I returned to the office.
Not for work.
Not for closure.

But because I had one last act of joy to offer:
A cake.

A simple celebration.
One I knew she wouldn't plan for herself.

And so we cut the cake.
Smiles. Laughter.
At least on the surface.

But beneath it, I felt it—

That quiet shift in her spirit.
The emotional step backward she hadn't yet admitted to herself.

She didn't sense it.
But I did.

Because when you've been emotionally intimate with someone,
you don't need them to speak.
You just feel the gap grow where warmth once lived.

I didn't ask questions.
I didn't force a moment.

But I knew what was coming.

The block.
The silence.
The emotional wall wrapped in logic and practicality.

It was her way of **coping**.
Of building emotional distance disguised as maturity.

And still—

I didn't give up.

Because I knew something she didn't:

This job wasn't just a new chapter.

It was the start of her **healing.**

A way out of the noise.
Out of the manipulation.
Out of the expectations forced on her by others.

And maybe one day—when the dust settled—
she would finally **hear what I had been saying all along**.

Not in words.
But in the way I always showed up.

So I continued asking her for one thing— **her reply.**

Not because I needed a yes.
But because I needed **her to confront what she had buried.**

To look at the bond we had and decide—

Was it real?
Or was it something she let go of just to make others comfortable?

I was ready to be blocked.
To be forgotten.
To be misunderstood.

But I wasn't ready to let her walk away
without knowing what it feels like to be truly, unconditionally chosen.

Because one day, when she finds the silence to think clearly, maybe she'll remember:

I wasn't the one who left.
I was the one who stayed,
even as the door slowly closed.

●●●

Chapter 30

State to State, Soul to Soul

"When love becomes truth, you stop asking for permission to care.
You simply show up—
not to change their decision,
but to honor the soul that once gave you strength."

I had stepped into a new role.

A bigger one. A bolder one.

Regional Head — Gujarat
Assistant Manager designation.
A new state. A new rhythm.
More responsibility, more accountability— and far less time for wishful thinking.

But still…

Some people don't live in your calendar.
They live in your heartbeat.

And for me, that person was still **her**.

Komal had received her posting too—

Deputy Manager in Assam.

A title well-deserved.

A challenge she had earned.

But her **last working day** was still a month away.

And in that space of transition— I saw something she couldn't:

The emotional baggage she was planning to carry along would only slow down the very growth she claimed to chase.

So I began.

Not by chasing.

But by confronting.

The **walls she had built—**

boundaries she thought would protect her, but were only protecting her confusion.

The logic she clung to was no longer valid. The fears she hid behind were already broken.

The silence she weaponized… only proved how loud the truth had become.

You cannot build a new life

by denying the heart that helped you escape the last one.

And so she did what many do when they feel emotionally cornered—

She blocked me.

Everywhere.

Messages.

Calls.

Every platform where emotion could leak through.

But love doesn't require Wi-Fi.
It requires **willingness**.

And I still had mine.

Her farewell day arrived.

A room full of colleagues gathered, everyone watching, listening as she tried to express her parting thoughts.

But something in her speech was… off.

She said things that didn't quite land.
Statements laced with emotion, but lacking coherence.

Some smiled awkwardly.
Some exchanged glances.
Most thought: *"What is she even saying?"*

But I stood there, still.

Because **I understood.**

Her words weren't making sense because they weren't words—

they were emotions desperately trying to find shape.

And I knew those emotions.

Because I had carried them once, too.

That panic of letting go.
That confusion between strength and sadness.
That ache of pretending you're fine when your soul is shaking.

And just when the day was over, another twist appeared—
her train ticket wasn't confirmed.

Some called it bad planning.
Some blamed the system.

But I saw it differently.

Sometimes the universe delays not to inconvenience, but to offer ***alignment.***

And without hesitation,

I walked with her—

to the station, to the platform, to the moment.

I made a few calls, spoke to a few railway officials, adjusted what I had to, and made sure she got on that train **with dignity.**

Not because she asked.

But because she deserved that.

Even if she didn't speak to me.

Even if she was still blocking the very hand that steadied her.

And then… something strange happened.

As she stood inside the train,

right in front of me,

a **call came to my phone.**

It was from **her number.**

But she hadn't called.

Her phone was in her bag.

She was looking right at me.

I didn't say anything.

I didn't need to.

Because I had seen this kind of thing before.

The Universe.

Calling.

Confirming what the soul already knows.

And as the train finally began to move—
it stopped again.

Not for a signal.
Not for traffic.

Just… paused.
As if time was giving us one last look,
one last whisper:

"This isn't over."

She didn't look back.
But I did.

Not in regret.
But in recognition—

That even if she had blocked me…
The universe hadn't.

Even if she'd turned away…
Love hadn't.

And even if this chapter was closing for her,
I had shown up—not for attention, but for **peace**.

For her.
And for myself.

●●●

Chapter 31

Four Months Later

"Sometimes, what hurts isn't just the silence.
It's that the silence came after a week of soft understanding—
a glimpse of what could've been,
right before it was taken away."

Four months had passed since I asked her the most sacred question of my life:

"Will you marry me?"

And in that time, I never rushed.
I never reminded her of timelines.
I simply stayed —
in spirit, in presence, in quiet commitment.

Then came her **last working day.**
A new chapter for her was opening, and I wanted to be part of closing the previous one—

not for my sake,
but for her peace.

I helped her walk out with grace,
not noise.
Not confusion.

And for a while…
it seemed like something had **shifted.**

In the **week that followed**,
we spoke more freely.
No tension.
No judgment.
Just two people reconnecting through truth.

There was **understanding**.
There was **comfort**.

It wasn't loud.
But it was **real**.

She laughed again.
She listened again.
She allowed me in again.

And for the first time in a long while,
I began to believe—
maybe she really meant it when she said:

"Give me 12 months."

But just as that belief began to take root,
everything fell apart.

No fight.
No warning.
Just silence.

Followed by a block.

Then another.

And another.

Until every way I could reach her was **gone.**

No one else would've seen it coming.

But I did.

Because I've known her deeply—

her fears, her patterns, her need to feel in control when the emotions become too much.

Her body had softened around me during that week. Her spirit was open again.

But her **mind—**

it couldn't handle the **truth that was returning**.

And so it did what minds like hers are trained to do when scared—

Shut down the heart.

Blocking me wasn't about punishment.

It was about panic.

That week we shared—it brought her closer to herself.

Closer to what she tried to deny.

And that's exactly why she had to cut the cord.

Because her soul had felt something again.

And her ego wasn't ready to deal with it.

So once again, I stood in the echo of someone I never stopped loving.

This time not from rejection,

but from a **fear that dressed itself as logic.**

No closure.
No "I'm not ready."
No farewell.

Just disappearance.
Just distance.
Just digital voids where conversations once bloomed.

But here's the truth:

I don't regret that week.
If anything, I'm grateful.

Because for those seven days—
I had her back.
Not entirely. Not forever.
But in that space, I saw the woman I always believed in.

And if loving someone means holding space for both their growth and their fear,
then I did that well.

She may have blocked me.
She may have walked away before the 12th month ever arrived.
But I still carry what we shared—

Not the silence she left behind…
But the spark she tried to extinguish
because she wasn't ready to burn that brightly again

•••

Chapter 32

The Email That Freed Me

"Some conversations are never finished.
They simply pause inside a person forever.
And sometimes, the only closure you'll ever get...
is the truth you choose to write."

After all the messages were blocked,
after the silence grew loud,
after I was erased from every platform where we once laughed, argued, healed—
there was only **one space left** where my voice could still reach her:
Email.

And I knew...
this was going to happen.

That she would eventually retreat into silence,
either out of fear or fatigue.

So I had already chosen the most complete way to speak to her: **with written truth.**

The email wasn't a goodbye.
It wasn't even an explanation.

It was **my final act of love—**
through clarity, honesty, and courage.

In it, I didn't repeat the things we had already talked about.
Those conversations would now live within her— etched in memory, not in inboxes.

Instead, I laid out **everything I had never been allowed to explain fully**:
Why I did what I did.
Why I stayed silent sometimes.
Why I stepped ahead sometimes.
Why I teased, encouraged, protected, and even withdrew when I had to.

I put everything on the table.
Every intention. Every decision. Every emotion.

And I wrote it all **with grace.**

But in the process…
something broke inside me.

A part I didn't think could still be wounded—
was wounded.

Because somewhere in her words,
she questioned something sacred to me— my **upbringing**.

She said what I had survived wasn't enough to justify who I was.
She questioned how I became this version of myself,

as though my struggles and resilience weren't valid.

And that shook something deep inside—
The **giver** in me.
The part that always went the extra mile for people
—not because they asked, but because I *understood* what they couldn't say.

That one comment made me do something I'd never done before:
Reevaluate how I give.

Not because I became bitter.
But because **even love must have boundaries**.

From that moment on, I decided:

- I will no longer go deep into people who only speak in silence.
- I will only help those who show up for themselves too.
- I will no longer pour from a cup someone keeps knocking over.

And maybe…
that was the real closure.

Not her reply.
Not her acceptance.
But the moment I stopped letting people break the very part of me
that was always trying to build them up.

And so, I sent her this final letter—

not to win her back,
but to let her know who I truly was.

That behind the teasing was tenderness.
Behind the strategy was protection.
Behind the silence was love.

Chapter 33

The Final Letter

"This wasn't a love letter.
This wasn't a confession.
This was a farewell written not in pain,
but in clarity."

After all that had happened—
the waiting,
the silence,
the brief return,
and the quiet vanishing—
I chose not to knock again.

I chose to write.

Not to justify.
Not to plead.

But to **document the truth**—mine.
And to offer her a mirror she was too afraid to look into.

This letter wasn't a cry for attention.

It was a calm voice from the deepest part of me saying:

"Even if you don't understand now,
you'll know one day I stood by you fully,
and left only when I had said it all."

Here is the full content of that letter—unedited, unfiltered, and completely from the soul.

The Final Email

Hi Komal,

Yesterday, what you said was right about my upbringing— that I didn't get the love of my parents when I needed them the most. But you have to remember… I never wished for that. I never prayed to God to take my mother.

You don't know what it feels like to lose your mother just as you enter the 9th standard… and to not receive the love from your father that you so desperately need.

You don't know the feeling of having no one to hold your hand in your ups and downs.

But I rose.

I overcame.

I rebuilt myself.

Life taught me not through comfort, but through storms.

And because of that, I've always led with love and care— especially for those I sensed were carrying wounds they didn't know how to show.

I gave what I never received.

That's the only way I know how to live.

You once told me that teasing and abusing is childish. But to me, that was the most raw form of affection between people who knew how to love beyond formalities.

That's how I encouraged people. That's how I challenged them to grow. That's how I pushed them out of their comfort zone.

And with you, I did it even more.
Because I saw more in you than you allowed yourself to admit.

I am talkative.
I am creative.
I am protective.
I am intuitive.

And I stayed one step ahead—not to control you, but to **guide you silently.**

I saw your dreams, even when you didn't voice them.
I noticed the smallest things—like when you talked about your eyes, or your wish to return to Kanpur.
And I never forgot them.

I laid your roadmap.
Quietly. Softly. Carefully.
Because I knew you needed things in steps, not all at once.

And yes… I liked you.
Not just for your eyes.
But for your boldness.
Your truth.
Your contradictions.

But I never told you everything.
Because **you weren't ready to meet all of me.**

You asked for maturity.

I gave it.
You asked for understanding.
I became it.

But in the end…
You judged my upbringing.

And that changed everything.

That comment broke something inside me.
A part that never expected to be questioned—
the part that gave selflessly, that loved deeply,
that never asked for anything in return except space to care.

From that day onward, I drew a line.
I stopped helping in silence.
I stopped diving deep into those who couldn't recognize my intentions.
I built boundaries—not out of anger,
but out of **self-respect**.

And yet… I don't hate you.
I never will.

Because you were one of my greatest teachers.
Not in how to love… but in how to **protect my own heart**.

You helped me grow in ways you'll never understand.
You shaped parts of me that now feel unshakable.

And no, I'm not a boy.
I may be 26, but life made me walk like I'm 32.

So I leave you with this:

Never mock someone's parvarish.
Because the boy who lost his mother at 14

has been holding onto her last words as his only dream ever since.

And if nothing else...
respect the story you never took time to read.

Take care,
Umang Ahuja

This was not a letter written out of heartbreak.
It was written from **resolution**.

It didn't ask for her return.
It didn't wish her guilt.
It didn't beg for understanding.

It simply said:
This is who I was.
This is what I gave.
And this is what I learned.

I never heard back.
But that's okay.

Some messages aren't meant to be replied to.
They're meant to **echo in the soul**,
when the person is finally ready to hear them.

And maybe she will.
Maybe she won't.
But I did my part.

And from this letter onward,

I no longer seek closure.
I carry **completion**.

Acknowledgements

"No story is written alone.

This one was carried by love, loss, silence, and the strength that comes from both support and absence."

To my Mother –

Though you left when I had just stepped into manhood, your absence became my greatest teacher.

You taught me love by making me search for it in every corner of life.

This book carries your memory in every page.

And every word I've written has been touched by the part of me that still wishes you were here.

To my Father –

You tried to give me the love of both parents.

And even when you fell short, I now understand — that too, was love in its own way.

You gave me resilience, and for that, I am forever grateful.

To my Sister –

Even the distance and misunderstandings shaped me.

They taught me how to love without expectations — and that's a powerful kind of love.

To the girl I first loved –

Thank you for teaching me that love cannot be forced, and that silence sometimes holds more meaning than words.

You were my first heartbreak, and you showed me the strength of letting go.

To the roommate and his sister –

That chapter taught me about hope, jealousy, and learning to see through the cracks.

Even pain adds to the foundation of who we become.

To Mr. Ajay Sharma –

You didn't just believe in my work — you believed in *me*.

Thank you for recognizing my clarity, giving me trust, and treating me like a younger brother when I needed it the most.

You helped turn responsibility into leadership.

To Mr. P. –

Thank you for the motivation, the recognition, and for seeing the leader in me before I saw it myself.

Your belief pushed me to take full accountability — and that changed everything.

To the friend I helped place in my company –

You reminded me what brotherhood in friendship means. Helping you was never a favor — it was a reflection of the bond we built.

To Komal –

This book wouldn't exist without you.

You were the spark, the stillness, the trigger, and the teacher.

You helped me come out of habits I was drowning in, without ever preaching a word.

Your silence and smile gave me healing, and your distance gave me depth.

I never hated you. I only hoped you'd find what I once saw in you — and maybe, still do.

Our journey may not have ended how I once wished, but it gave me a story that saved me.

To Those Who Tried to Break Me — Thank You.

To the one who manipulated — you showed me deception. From that, I chose clarity.

To those who left, blocked, or misunderstood — you reminded me that distance isn't always rejection. Sometimes, it's redirection.

And I'm better for it.

To Everyone Who Stayed –

Your presence was my anchor.

Thank you for standing beside me, even in my silences.

And finally, to the Reader –

If you've made it this far, thank you.

May this story remind you that being broken doesn't mean you're weak —

it means you're *in the process of becoming whole.*

With all my heart,
Umang Ahuja

Epilogue

I Didn't Lose Her, I Found Myself

"What began as a story of love
ended as a story of awakening.
And that, too, is a love story—
but this time, with myself."

There was a time I gave without pause.
Without boundaries.
Without needing to be understood.

Because I believed love was enough.
That giving was healing.
That staying was loyalty.

But this journey—these 33 chapters—
taught me something else.

That love without direction is exhaustion.
That giving without asking is depletion.
That loyalty to pain is not growth—

it's self-abandonment.

I didn't write this book to change the past.
I wrote it to **understand it**.
To honor the boy who lost his mother but never stopped mothering others.
To forgive the young man who let silence replace his own voice.
To salute the leader in me who rose without a title
and chose peace over politics.
And to let go of the version of me
who waited for someone else's acceptance
before accepting himself.

Komal will always be a part of this story.
Not because she stayed—
but because **she showed me who I become when I love deeply**.

And in doing so,
she helped me meet the man I was always meant to be.

A man who now gives with discernment.
Who leads with balance.
Who helps, but no longer at the cost of his own soul.

I no longer chase closure.
I **create it**.
I no longer seek answers from people who don't ask questions.
I find them in my own silence.

And in that silence,
I've heard the clearest voice of all:

"You didn't lose her.
You were simply guided back to yourself."

So here I am.
Standing tall.
Grateful.
At peace.

With no hate in my heart.
Only memories, lessons, and a deeper kind of love—
the kind I now give to **me first.**

This is not the end.
This is the foundation.
Of a better life,
a better love,
a better me.

Final Message

"This book is for every soul who has ever loved unconditionally, given without asking, and stayed long after they were understood."

To the ones who were silenced, misunderstood, or walked away feeling empty—

know this:

You were never broken. You were being rebuilt.

You were never abandoned. You were being realigned.

The sacrifices you made, the love you gave, and the hope you held onto—

they are not wasted.

The universe has not forgotten your heart.

So never stop believing in the power of love, even if it didn't return the way you expected.

Never stop trusting the process, even when you can't see the end.

And above all—

Never lose hope.

Because the universe always finds a way to bring you to the version of yourself that was worth all the waiting, all the pain, and all the love you gave away.

You didn't come this far to be left empty.

You came this far to finally become **whole**.

About the Author

Umang Ahuja is not just a name, but a journey — of resilience, emotional courage, and silent leadership. Raised in the absence of a mother and shaped by the emotional distance of a father, he grew up learning to carry pain quietly and turn it into purpose.

A telecom professional by designation and a giver by nature, Umang's life has been a testament to what it means to rise when no one is watching. From becoming a beloved school leader to designing national telecom rollouts, from surviving heartbreak to rediscovering his voice in silence — every phase of his life is driven by a deep sense of emotional integrity and quiet strength.

The Second Chance I Gave Myself is his first book — a deeply personal narrative that chronicles the emotional scars, silent sacrifices, and breakthroughs of a young man who loved, lost, and finally chose to love himself. It's more than a memoir. It's a mirror for anyone who's ever loved deeply and forgotten to choose themselves in the process.

Today, Umang continues to lead not just through his profession, but through his story — one that reminds others that it's never too late to begin again, and that sometimes, **the greatest love story is the one you write with yourself.**